Thursdays

Camilla Eustance

BookLeaf Publishing

Presentation by *BookLeaf Publishing*

Web: www.bookleafpub.com

E-mail: info@bookleafpub.com

ISBN: 9789357614443

First edition 2022

ACKNOWLEDGEMENT

I acknowledge and pay my respects to the Traditional Custodians of the land and waterways on which I work and live, the Wurundjeri Woi Wurrung people of the Kulin Nations. This is stolen land and sovereignty has never been ceded. Always was, always will be Aboriginal land.

The bell goes on ringing

It matters not the music
nor the time of day

Because this keeps happening
over and over

I check, you check,
we turn around &
everyone's checking

Call it an alarm, a song, a whisper

Something goes on ringing

You could say it's insidious
but maybe it's just obvious

We can't fall off the wall,
down the well, to the sea

We are in its midsts always

Tablecloth blue, tablecloth white,
no table at all
it's there

Birds walking over it,
rubbish accumulating around it

No clock-work-bent-down-body-work it
will
stay it will pace
the halls
of your brain

Of your/in your heart,

That subtle ping, a trill
deep in the inner ear

The bell
goes on ringing.

As I said

As I said,
evolution doesn't have
to be linear

I was born here
This is my Grandmother's pen

She has lived a life of criticism
swirling around her
through the 30s, 40s, 50s, 60s,
70s, 80s, 90s, & now

Arrows directed inwards,
pinning her to duty
and the eternal feeling of
not being enough

Still, as she sits, staring

Her beauty, her strength
shines like sunlight
piercing a cloud

Those bright, bright
blue eyes

As I said, it's not
linear

But that is strength
behind her eyes

And it is travelling down the line

Bird

In this old city, the pigeons circle me gently

You came here too with the powerful bird on
your chest
Breathing with you
Concealed under an orange t-shirt

I wake in the dark at four most mornings
Spluttered to consciousness by stories where
you're still just a block away
Now, at six, my eyes open a little wider

It's eight now
And it's been light for an hour
Avian trills echo in my coffee cup

My friend said when she saw you,
He just looked like he was having a lovely nap

I'm not sure if she said lovely - I may have
added that in,
Hoping

At least I know that it was a relief for you to get
to sleep

Maybe that will calm my breathing down just enough
For me to do so too, in ten hours' time

And then wake up again
Watch the morning birds flying past outside

All of this beauty, and

You sleep
But the pigeon on your chest is dreaming

"Is this your paint?"

Yes, and it's my pain too

Search for the first instance of Louisa

Where will you search for the relevant grey
literature?
(Your next lesson is on searching the grey
literature)

This appointment occurs in the past

She is eye opening to touch,
the dead space has not finished emptying by the
time the next inspiration comes along

To this end, compose a short biography
Consider in your answer the work of breathing

Insufficient evidence:

Failure to sense
Failure to capture
Failure to pace

Search for the first instance of Louisa

November 2017

I was sitting in the fluorescent lights,
    no, underneath them.
Definitely underneath them.

With all these others,
     a myriad of black sandals /
country road shirts / caps / grey arm hair
and three quarter length cargo pants.

I worried, through my damp socks
hiding the blisters from my shiny damp shoes
that my shorts - also damp -
were too short.

     My gold hoops too big,
my achievements too scant
for this serious Crowd.

Gathering in celebration of an archive
of a poet who I had never met
and barely knew.

Every time it was time to clap
I lowered my champagne glass
very, very carefully

on to the
wooden floor

Terrified that it would be knocked
out of my hand
by some unknown gust of something,
the air-conditioning, maybe

Or that it would make a
large, clumsy clunk onto the floor

Whilst a sombre voice
read the mumbling, undulating
verse of the dead poet.

Everyone would look at me,

Frowning, perhaps, and
think
   What's she doing here?

I stared furiously at the
corner of the Aboriginal artwork
on the wall, and then the space
between that and the skylight
   to keep myself from
emitting   anything

A sound, a shuffle, an out-of-place tear

As this man's beautiful words
cut at the angles of the chairs
we were sitting on,

And as both the words
and the downpour I'd been caught in
        sank right through my clothes
                into my skin.

Endless

In the corner of my field of hearing I can hear the endless rustle of plastic bags being filled. It doesn't change, and day and night, it's exactly the same lighting. The only thing that changes are the shoppers coming and going. And the occasional drilling or beeps. Or that sound, like the hammering of tent pegs from long ago.

When your chatbot reaches a leaf

and you can't find a condition that evaluates to
true
no special anything_else condition
that always evaluates to true

(On the top left, it is Secret)

random forest

This week we have only one dot:
• Quality
and
This should create a new variable called
OverallAnxiety

View(ToothGrowth)
continuing with our skewness,

Watch: The zooming out movie
"everything is related to everything else, but
near things are more related than distant things"

Drive is to Drove as Dive is to Dove
approximately Normal

How to run one way and two way
The package is loaded and ready.

heart$AC <- NULL

At The Dinner

15

Waiting for that moment in that song.
Feeling awkward that their relationship isn't the
same as it used to be but knowing it's not
entirely her fault. Hoping that they'll be others,
and not just him, at the dinner.

The Bus

The light from the bus
runs red and blue
it's cheap,
but it's beautiful

Though I can't pretend that I like it
when we leave two hours late

Sun going down among these cars
when will yours?

Maybe if you install yourself permanently
in front of your black screen
it never will -
mind you, you're not far off at this point

And the distractions aren't slowing down

As long as the corporations that govern you
keep clinking their champagne glasses

You life in one perpetual blue-lit rectangle

Sorry - not in, *is*.

The bears, the bats, the trees
calling you

But you've been clamping mechanics
on your ear drums and eyeballs
as long as they've existed

And I hate you for it, for what you're doing
to you, your brain and your home.

Maybe I just need to find the teacher, the parent,
the adult

Who
forgot to tell you
that this world is shared.

Shared. But look, with a little carelessness;
a bump on the road when you're texting
that changes the appearance of the letter -

You assume the world is meant to be Shaved.

Maybe you're not even thinking about it,
swilling assumptions that don't even get
the luxury of being acknowledged

If everything is on the screen,
it only lasts 65 seconds, 2 minutes max

and that timing, contrary to that of this bus,

Has bled into you.

All around you exists in simulacra, if this is your
way of existing.

There is a baby over there
(she is gorgeous)
I could almost cry for the world that she doesn't
know yet

Keep it that way,
don't let her be crushed like the rest of us

Unless she can find those
glittering moments
in between the flat pixels

The bus will never move out of this polluted
city.

vaccine poem

Exceedingly Bright
a centre for huge grey machines

where we come and sit far apart
removed from each other
on our own machines

The needle was huge but it didn't hurt as much
as I expected

and for some it didn't hurt at all

"you must be thick-skinned", i said
to the person sitting 1.5m behind me

There's a tiny box of glass hidden in the wall

It looks where a businessman would sit,
endlessly updating a spreadsheet

Meanwhile his assistant would bring him a
sandwich, the same every day at precisely noon

Back to my black chair among 300 other
identical chairs

the humdrum of a global pandemic
a global panic

rendered in monochrome, threaded into our
newsfeeds, factored into every decision we make
when we step onto the footpath

it stings but it's probably worth it

Arms Up

The past trails away
The irrelevant past

I don't, I like to think,
Do that anymore:
Hold my arms up
For the impossible past

I just want to keep
Writing poetry in the car,
about now, about the present

In the presence
Of fleeting gums and bins and fields
And people who will stay

Maybe, nah, fuck that
I was going to say:
Maybe you too, (I hope you'll stay)

But that's another poem
I'm not writing that poem right now

Overhung

I'm splayed on the carpet
a bad-mannered starfish clutching my toes

Half a piece of toast hangs from my mouth like
an old bauble on a Christmas tree
my hair is seaweed,
dancing in
greasy, disgusting tangles around my neck

In ten minutes I will
stand in the shower and dissolve,
skull against the tiles
for now I'll just lie back on these crumbs

Last night
sloshing around my head like
soggy gym shoes thrown from a car

The scraps keep appearing
churning out groans like a compost bin

I plummeted from the dance floor
onto a pair of eyelinered fish heads
sucking out each other's gills in time to Kanye,
swaggering nasty through the throng

I think I smiled clumsily and retrieved politely
the slice of lime
that had fallen on her head from my glass

Then, failing to care, I flailed my jelly arms
back into the strobe light wonderland of
whoever's kitchen it was

My toast is as soggy as the gym shoes now
I must have dribbled into its charred, miserable
crusts

Where's mum?

There was this other bit where
I was talking to the wall and you came up
behind me
putting one drink in my hand, one hand on my
waist
my silly drunk waist

I turned around to your grin, and all the noise
stopped
my eyes lolled from the bridge of your Roman
nose to the sharp line of your chin to your neck
and I grinned back, foolish like a schoolgirl
but there was…something

Until, in the shaky blur
you were gone, replaced by a fridge
and I realised I was standing
head over the sink
alone

A Wave

A shell lies waiting
beaming in a ray of light
(my hand)

We lie in a hot room
smiling around the curl
of the shell

Bright blue, a day away
and a dream
falling

In the thick of the last night
I sang to the shell
the melody ran in a wink

Trailed off into the heaving sea
there's no more
and I'm on a plane

And suddenly what I had is gone
disappeared

(a wave)

Flies

All day long, away from the cloudy wind
grabbing flies from the air

Absurd irritation in their dizzying dance
and so rude,
the small and silent attack
on personal space

Poetry works when small and large things
are put in dialogue

Like my hand on this page, or me in this house
and the flies around my face

Is that rain?

This day, like others in the house
away from the wind
is filled with small plotlines

Squashed by a clap of the hands in an hour
as the pen scribbles out the point

Plotline, space, plotline, space
one fly killed, space, ten flies killed

A walk around the block
(a purpose slotted into a space)

The flies appear aimless, but they're not

I appear full of purpose, but

I find
the day whittled away
with only squashed flies to show for it.

Years From Now and Long Since

(part one)

It was only everything.

Big blue of sleep he was
the sweet warm father

Blinking at dawn
with a seagull cry

Once a sailor far away
now when I am still awake at four,

He's there in black and white
weeping small on our fridge

As I drink a cup from the wall
standing by steering-wheel musk

The still sink dark is
bright lit new

Or bright lit gone

Falling far from him, he's the faded man
in his old newspaper town

Bread under his arm
spreading the rainy streets
just pixels or is it

The pale white of a storybook
expiring quietly
but never really changing

(part two)

Staying on the soaked verandah
in the red land

With dropped oranges
and forgotten pencils

A neighbour quietly checking
        no,
she's left already

Years ago maybe

Back when the children were in bed
before the wine and the cold

and the mess
of the night before

I remembered briefly, meekly
the shadow of the plates

The way his fork lay restless on the cloth
and the freshly cut scars

But the froth of the waves
when we were free and when
we were in pain

Among the facts, the factories
joy from lined meadows
swept me and

Him and the man
from across

Picture book or pictorial or picked
it's smashed
into a hundred whisky-soaked stones
it's

Too far out of bed to say I miss
So we step past

Fall away

with repetition of blue and red

Chipped now
chipped back then

The great big bird
who stole it all,
had stolen it all from the beginning

(part three)

You look at me tired, neutral
blank
under the inappropriate lighting

Never to know free form
but with eyebrows turned up

and practicality speaks

Has spoken,
thus claims
the puddle in which my chair turns round and
round

nonsense or none
the floral corridors I tend to pace down

or go gracefully
on wheels of air

I can't even hear the creak anymore
I'm leaking from the head downwards and

They'll never know

It was only everything.

Wondering where

She hasn't overcome the self-centeredness of being a teenager yet, nor the childishness you can almost always get away with at that age. The hairbrush anecdote - talking, ironically, (in this context) about how people perceive themselves to be complete at any given point in their lives... then she just interrupted by saying how knotty her hair tends to be, then the kind of hairbrush she likes to use, then the shops she likes to buy them from. I looked at her with weak, glazed-over eyes. I was looking past her, wondering where the interesting, interrupted conversation had gone.

bunnings

34

children's music for adults
a sea of roofs and nothing to do
she's her own peculiar brand of weird
i can get through this cold this day this mood
bushland bushland
tiny hairs on the back of my hands
a confused longing for something else
loads of birds on a bench
now we're in the car
now we're on the highway
we have already passed three different bunnings
this weak thread of inspiration slipping away the
further from the trees we get

Vietnam Haiku I,II,III

The monsoon evening
dripped slow on my collarbone
dripped fast on my feet

I choked on the Bánh
she misunderstood and laughed
I just looked around

The sun is setting
Vietnam blushes red
quiet, I think: you

The Rose-peddler

Out on my own, I drive
through the sticky semen night

I write, and who do I write to?

It's that person at the back of the queue, the one
whose head never turns around
who holds their gaze steadfast in the other
direction

They've been given so many roses,
and never accepted a single one

As I slow down at the lights,
a crow catches the wheel
and there's the terrible crunch

The car behind me sees my shock
in the rearview mirror

I barely have it in me
to notice the flowers slide off the dashboard
onto the passenger seat floor

I cleaned it last week, but now
it feels dirtier than ever

The Jarrah Table

At night I don't hear the whales anymore

they used to sing, and float
magnificent,
translucent
around the foot of my bed

or around the caves in my head

so I could always sleep
in the truth of home.

Tap the piano keys. Bang them,
place your entire palms on the rectangular ivory
fingers
and crash, explode your feelings out

in a glorious, cathartic drone

Please, bring me back
to the steady 5 o'clock days
where my father's thoughts
echoed in notes

around the shadows in our house

and in the shadows hiding,
content

under the solid Jarrah table.

I rejoice in a group
of four knitted souls
brought together by candles
and a meal

I now think of three,
and it makes my face crumple

Like the paper I threw away
every time I tried
to write myself
a letter.
So now, now that I am more
than a mere crescent moon

but less than full

it's all I can do, some evenings,
to pick up the prettiest autumn leaves

and hold them tender
in my two pockets,
clutching also

to a postcard from Paris in the 60's

whilst

The apple crumble topping, sits,
pleasantly humming with flavour

reminding me of ovens, your hugs
Hermione the cat

and the thick, magnanimous
grape vine
wrapping its arms around us

every day of the year.

www.ingramcontent.com/pod-product-compliance
Lightning Source LLC
Chambersburg PA
CBHW070613160726
48003CB00005B/2255